12050

11/05   17

Turtles

ABDO
Publishing Company

A Buddy Book
by
Julie Murray

VISIT US AT
www.abdopub.com

Published by Buddy Books, an imprint of ABDO Publishing Company, 4940 Viking Drive, Suite 622, Edina, Minnesota 55435. Copyright © 2003 by Abdo Consulting Group, Inc. International copyrights reserved in all countries. No part of this book may be reproduced in any form without written permission from the publisher.

Printed in the United States.

Edited by: Christy DeVillier
Contributing Editors: Matt Ray, Michael P. Goecke
Graphic Design: Maria Hosley
Image Research: Deborah Coldiron
Photographs: Animals Animals, Digital Stock, Digital Vision Ltd., Minden Pictures, Photodisc

Library of Congress Cataloging-in-Publication Data

Murray, Julie, 1969-
    Turtles/Julie Murray.
        p. cm. — (Animal kingdom (Edina, Minn.))
    Summary: Provides simple information about the physical characteristics, habits, and different kinds of turtles.
    ISBN 1-57765-720-9
        1. Turtles—Juvenile literature. [1. Turtles.] I. Title. II. Series.

QL666.C5 M86 2002
597.92—dc21

2001056065

Contents

Turtles Are Reptiles

Turtles are **reptiles**. Reptiles have scaly skin. Turtles have scales on their head, legs, and tail. Snakes, lizards, crocodiles, and alligators are reptiles, too.

Turtles and other reptiles are **ectothermic** animals. Ectothermic animals cannot make heat inside their bodies. Turtles lie in the sun to heat themselves. They become slow when they are too cold.

Crocodiles, lizards, snakes, alligators, and turtles are reptiles.

Turtles have been around for more than 200 million years.

What Turtles Look Like

Turtles can be many sizes. Some turtles only weigh three pounds (one kg). Some turtles weigh 1,500 pounds (680 kg). Leatherback turtles grow to be about eight feet (two m) long. The eastern bog turtle only grows to be about three inches (eight cm) long.

Turtles are the only **reptiles** with a shell. A turtle's shell may be black, brown, green, or yellow. Some turtles can pull their head, legs, and tail inside their shell. This helps to keep them safe from enemies.

8

A turtle's shell is part of its body.

Freshwater Turtles

There are over 100 kinds of freshwater turtles. Mud turtles, painted turtles, and softshell turtles are freshwater turtles. They live in lakes, rivers, and ponds. Some freshwater turtles live on land, too.

Freshwater turtles have **webbed** feet. Webbed feet help turtles swim.

A freshwater turtle

Some freshwater turtles bury themselves in mud during winter. They sleep, or **hibernate**, there until spring.

Tortoises

Tortoises are land turtles. They live in jungles, forests, and deserts. There are about 50 kinds of tortoises.

The leopard tortoise lives in Africa. This tortoise does not **hibernate**.

The pancake tortoise has a flatter shell than other tortoises. It can squeeze itself into small places.

Leopard tortoise

Pancake tortoise

Most tortoises sleep inside a **burrow**. The gopher tortoise can dig a 25-foot (8-m) burrow. It stays there during the hot part of the day. Snakes, mice, or toads may share the gopher tortoise's burrow. Some tortoises **hibernate** in their burrows during the winter.

Gopher tortoise

Are All Turtles Slow?

Not all turtles are slow like tortoises. Freshwater turtles and sea turtles can swim fast. Sea turtles can swim as fast as 18 mph (29 kph).

Sea Turtles

Sea turtles are some of the biggest turtles. They live in all oceans except the Arctic Ocean. They use their **flippers** for swimming.

Some sea turtles travel very far to lay eggs. They go to the same beach where they were hatched. A sea turtle may travel thousands of miles to get there.

Sea turtles live
in the ocean.

Eating

Tortoises mostly eat plants. Some sea turtles eat jellyfish, crabs, and other sea animals. Some sea turtles eat sea grasses, too. Freshwater turtles eat plants, insects, fish, and snails.

Turtles do not have teeth. They bite with a sharp beak. Some turtles have long claws to rip open food.

Turtles eat with a sharp beak.

Turtle Babies

All turtles lay their eggs on land. A female turtle digs a hole to lay her eggs. Then, she covers the eggs up with sand, dirt, or leaves. Some turtles lay as many as 200 eggs.

Turtle eggs hatch after a few months. Baby turtles must dig their way out of the nest. Mother turtles do not take care of their babies. Turtle babies must learn to live on their own.

Turtles can live for a long time. Some turtles can live as long as 150 years!

A turtle's nest

Baby turtles

Important Words

burrow an animal's underground hole.

ectothermic describes animals that cannot make heat inside their bodies.

flippers the flat, paddle-shaped body parts that sea turtles use for swimming.

hibernate to spend the winter sleeping.

reptiles ectothermic animals with scales and a backbone.

webbed when toes are joined together with skin.

Web Sites

Kids' Questions about Turtles

www.micronet.net/users/~turtles/
pondfolder/kidspage/questions.html
Find out more about turtles here.

How Turtles Hibernate through the Winter

www.micronet.net/users/~turtles/
pondfolder/kidspage/hibernation.html
Learn more about turtle hibernation.

Kidz Korner

www.turtles.org/kids.htm
Read sea turtle stories and discover what you
can do to help sea turtles.

Index